Special thanks to my heavenly father for all

he has done. Thank you dad for sparking

my love of poetry and Trin for working

hard to illustrate my book. Thank you

Magic Jack and Spirit Thom for

mentoring me through this

whole process. I couldn't

have done it

without

you.

Elephant in the Room

"He left me because he was looking for his other half

and I wasn't her because I was whole all by myself."

The F* Word

So I like um wrote a poem because I'm like sick of older men

telling me I need to like

    -talk with confidence.

Maybe if you **paid attention** to what I had to say and stopped

degrading women,

I would have this confidence you speak of like

Don't tell me I need to put my vocabulary on a diet.

Supplement my words for your vocab plan

Weigh my *like* and *um's* on a scale so my language will be pretty

    -Meet societies standards of a perfect woman.

Wear makeup so a man can see I'm pretty enough to be

    tied

        down

            to.

As if my love is a prison sentence they took the plea bargain for.

I was asked why I wear makeup if I am already pretty.

Do you tell that to every girl you try to charm? Like

-Maybe she was born with it or maybe its Maybelline.

Like maybe she was born into societies cookie-cutter standards or

-maybe she spreads on her powder mask every morning

hoping she might be loved today

He told me I am too pretty to know what oppression means.

Too blonde to know who is running for president.

Too bubbly to know what it feels like to be discriminated against.

She wants the De... grading of women to stop

"Speak up and stop saying like and um so you can be respected"

he demands.

I didn't know that my um "extra words" like made me less of a

person because you can't seem to keep my word count in check.

Are you balancing my words like you balance my pay checks?

Do I get 77 words to your 100?

Are you budget cutting my language? Am I taking up too much of

your time? Can I veto the bill that limits my language to the

dictionary of the previous generations?

I will not let past bureaucrats lock up my tongue in the standard

testing textbooks they are feeding the

involuntary obese children today.

　　　-We bully them for being fat but

their free or reduced checkbooks' can only afford to taste the

thousand calorie meals we give them for school lunches.

"Sit down and shut up, this is a man's job"

　　　-they will say to my opinion.

But old man,

　　　　mark

　　　　　　my

words

I will be in the CEO chair of the company that puts your ego

-out of business.

I will evict you from your high horse and force you to watch me as I

rise to my throne. Crushing anyone who tells me I can't because

I'm like

too young

or too fragile

or I do it.

-Like a girl.

You could too

-if you tried **harder.**

My like and ums will be the rear view mirror I use to keep my

inferiors in my view. Let them not feel intimated by the bland

harsh words you are accustomed to,

-put my language in their hands so they can understand my

dialogs like an instruction manual and

be inspired to be the feminist revolution I will force to be revived.

-He gasps at the F word,

feminism

I can hear his mother tossing in her grave, remembering the hot

agonizing days she spent protesting for my rights but

His cigar and gentleman club buddies would not approve of a

-piece of meat

talking with such strong language to a man of *his* importance.

But that's what feminism is,

-strong.

Too many people think feminism is baggage, but its lighter than

the burden of my future in societies captivity.

There is a reason they made all the villains queens.

They are scared of our power.

Show

They have things to show of where they have spent their time but

There is little to nowhere where you can look at mine.

They show clay and lizards and things they have fed $\left(you\right)$ but

You can only look to where I stayed,

in my bed waiting until I fall through

I woke up this morning and walked down the stairs

sometimes it feels like I'm trying to fight bears

They have conversations and hugs to give you but

I only have this half faked smile and my presence too.

I can't wrap up my gift that I sprinkled with tears

I can't sift through my infinite undying fears

I want to have something to show but

When I don't I feel like I should just go.

I'm sorry I don't seem 100% present

I'm just trying to find acceptance

Shotgun Wedding

Who do you invite to a shotgun wedding?

I anxiously wait to see what names she trusts with her secret

She printed the guest list on the back of the napkin

    -she got from dinner

How do I tell her, her friends spilled slut on the invitation.

Told me three days isn't enough to pick out bridesmaid dresses

    -as if *that* was the issue

Checked plus one on the matte black glitter glue paper

    -her mama bought in bulk

A baby is a blessing. A baby you can love forever

But what do you do with a groom you cant plant your heart in

What if he can't build your love a home

How did he swallow the words baby and wedding in one gulp

What do you do to a 17 year young groom who's kisses have tainted

      all the bridesmaids

Did the groom wear black to camouflage with the barrel

of their shotgun themed smiles or to show his mourning?

Will he can his weeping in the sound suppressor?

Why don't they measure calibers in years?

What does he keep in his chamber of secrets

she has not yet unlocked

What skeletons does he tuck in at night?

Does he check the closet for his missing friends?

Does she taste the gunpowder in his kiss,

Did he engrave "I love you" on the trigger

What do you wear to a shotgun wedding?

Who's guilt should I wrap around my neck in the newest trend?

What shade of ghost do I power on my nose,

Conceal the gossip emerging from my thoughts

Use foundation so I remember to save some face,

Line my lips in respectful silence

If I wear falsies will I blend in with the crowd's smiles?

Can you wear white to a shotgun wedding?

What do you say to the bride of a shotgun wedding?

What apologetic beaded dress will she wear walking down the isle

    -of the public park gazebo

She pins a smile between her cheeks

    -so they don't see past her facade

Will she skip the line of objection?

      Who do you congratulate at a shotgun wedding?

Childhood Dreams

When I was a child, people always asked what I wanted to be

-when I grew up.

I didn't want to be a ballerina, cowgirl, or anything unrealistic.

Life took away my tippy cup and blankie and trained me to use big

girl panties. The kind without princesses on them.

"When I grow up" turned into "after college."

Which implies I need to attend college to grow up and that's

not true. Now when they ask mewhat I want to be, I say...

I want to be a cardiologist. I want to learn how to mend a broken

heart. I wanna learn how to stitch up the past and morph the

shattered pieces into a heart that will actually beat.

I want a Frankenstein heart made from pieces of everything I love

-but how can you make a heart out of nothing?

I want to be a doctor because doctors will know what's wrong with me. Can tell if my sadness is contagious. Prescribe me to a drug that will numb my emotions until I suture the gash they left in my innocence. I want to find a cure for the sickness that is living inside of me. I played operation as a kid.

-I have all the qualifications.

I can take the rope out from my neck with only tweezers and some hope. I still need to extract the butterflies in my stomach so they don't take over and cause me to fall in love.

I want to be an interpreter so I can teach people how to communicate with one another.

Change their words for the better.

Teach them the foreign language that I'm accustomed to.

11

Lesson One:

Fleek: nice looking

Bae: my lover

Gucci: of great quality

Selfie: a photography portrait of yourself

Please: a word used before a demand

Thank you: a word to soften your demands

Sorry: say this when they get upset.

Don't worry, it doesn't matter what promise you say next.

They will believe you regardless.

Promise: I might get around to it.

I want to be an astronaut so I don't have to live on this earth. I will

fly to the moon and examine the sun.

Hypothesis how it can shine so bright when it's surrounded by darkness. Why can't I shine so bright? I'm surrounded by darkness and black holes disguised as people. Sucking the life outta me with phrases like "be realistic" As a kid, I would wish upon the stars hoping they can shed some light on my life. But as I landed on the moon I realized the stars were dead, just like my dreams. I went to Jupiter to see if boys are really stupider but I realized I spent so much money to go to college to get more knowledge to get to space that I was the stupid one. Sitting alone in a dorm studying a world I can not experience. I need to get OUTTER this SPACE.

When I was younger I dreamed of becoming all these different people

      -so I didn't have to be me.

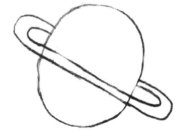

I am a Phantom

I haunt my own home with the memories of my sanity.

I wear all black to show them I'm sorry for their loss.

I mourn for the nights when I don't scream and scare them awake.

Most days I can walk around in broad daylight and no one seems to

notice me.

No one asks me how I slept because phantoms don't sleep and they

gave up on dreaming.

They don't ask me what my dreams are because they know my

dreams have became the scary background music I keep on loop to

remind me that my emotions change faster than the plot of Gillian

Flynn book.

Based on a true story rolls down the credits and everyone gasps.

The screen shows the name of everyone who worked to make the movie polished and clean so no one can see the dirty hands that

they placed in the directors chair

    -like some practical joke.

Like how can she be sad if she always seems happy?

How can she be broken if she can fix everyone else?

How can she be depressed if her life seems perfect?

The facts are bitter but they have sugar coated the ending so

people will spend money on the film.

    -because no one wants a movie about reality.

No one wants to stay to hear the truth.

No one wants to be my understudy

No one wants to play my part in the play.

No one wants to step in my footsteps and look I the ripples of my

mistakes and see the monster staring back at them.

No one wants to know I am not fine.

Birthday Wishes

When the strangers that share my bloodline asked my mom what I wanted for my birthday, I was disappointed that they didn't already know. Can't they tell I need more notebooks for the poems I passively aggressively write about them, that I am obsessed with cats, or noticed I have shared about 6 batman hoodies I have admired in the last month? Maybe they would see the patterns of all the following holiday gift wishes.

I should just tell them what I really want; no more guessing games.

I want a mirror for my room.

A haunted house mirror that might warp my reflection back into reality so I am not scared of the clown staring at me with her fake red smile, and baggy clothes that hide the body-in-construction.

I want a body that can't reflect more than 110 body points,

a body that diets on confidence that only comes from the big bad wolves that huff and puff me off my feet and into

-their hungry arms.

Lets get really crazy and ask for my innocence back or even

crazier, a YouTube app that will play songs even after the app is

closed.

Or perhaps a gift card to Amour so I could finally get that goodbye

kiss from my first love, I have been dreaming about it all these

years. A camera to show him, I can picture us together.

Can I have a remote to my life, so maybe I can rewind and warn

him about the waterfalls.

Don't pick up that rock, its too dangerous. You'll fall in and drown.

Or maybe fast forward past the funerals. But don't get me draw

string dolls that only say:

"I'm sorry for your loss, he's in a better place, he lived a good life,

this was apart of the big plan, Caleb was my friend."

Deceit slips off their tongues like a water slide down a mountain

I never asked to ride.

Maybe you can hire an excavator that will make new bloodlines so

you no longer have to claim me as family.

Maybe if they drain enough of my blood, I will develop amnesia

and forget that if you wanted to talk to me, you'd call, send me a

card, smoke signals, Morse code. I would learn Morse code if it

meant you might want to tell me

you love me.

But most of all, I just want something that tells me you still care.

Even if I know its a lie.

But as I notice your name on the

"Suggested friends" section on

Facebook, I realize you erased our

friendship with the click of a button months ago.

Queen of Disaster

I am the antagonist in my own film.

They call me queen but

      they don't know what that truly means.

I am the queen of downfall and dismay. I can make your funeral

look like an 8 year old girls dream wedding that they have been

planning for, for years.

This is a funeral your worst enemies would be *dying* to attend.

I am a queen waiting to be heard.

This stage is the only place where I can express my emotions

without feeling judgment or dismissal.

Maybe if I put a beautiful analogy on the deep demented plot they

will stay to watch the film.

      -But they will complain like all mortal peasants do

And I'm on too many diets to sugar coating anything.

So sit back, take a drink, SHUT UP and enjoy the show.

They say silence is the loudest scream so why can't you hear me screaming?

I'm laying down in the fetal position on my leather couch with the cinnamon-y scent of banana bread crisping in the kitchen spinning through the air just begging me to cheer up

    -but Adam's Song is playing on repeat through my headphone speakers and it overpowers the scent of comfort

    "Sixteen just held such better days, days when I could still feel alive we could wait until..." [Blink 182]

I stay silent, can you hear my screaming?

Waking up in a pool of sweat and drool to my mother telling me it was just a dream.

They say dreams come true but they forgot to mention that

    -my nightmares are dreams too.

It's the middle of the night I was literally screaming

    -Can you hear me yet?

When I scream, you're supposed to come to my rescue but

-Sometimes I don't scream.

Sometimes I ask politely.

Ask if I can get some magic beans that will grand me 3 magic

wishes and perhaps grow a giant

being stalk that help me discover who I am

-*being* versus who I want to be.

I repetitively ask if I can take a test [can I take a test? Can I take a

test?] to score how normal my emotions are.

-I am scared to get results that tell me I'm average.

Feeling ordinary means all this pain will continue and has the

potential to manifest. The little hope in me wishes that if I'm not

normal, then there is an

antidote to the spell that has castes upon me.

-Maybe there is a cure to my madness.

But we're all mad here, right?

~~The End~~

Wait wait wait.

The show isn't over.

I am the queen I get a fairytale ending. *"happily ever after"*,

     right?

-Wrong.

I lock the doors to my tower and hire a dragon to keep guard.

Destroy anyone who comes close so I don't destroy them first is

what I command of my scaly friend.Make sure no one falls for my

Medusa smile. Make sure no one looks into my chartreuse eyes and

sees that... I am beautiful.

Save the prince from me,

     don't let him see how charming and harmless I can seem.

As I wait in my castle for anyone who is willing to defeat my

dragon and break down my walls, I realize

I'm not the queen,

I'm just a damsel tired of her distress.

Society

We blame society but

we are the women that show our daughters

that we shouldn't be content with ourselves.

Pinching our fat with tears racing down our face

Powdering our nose to conceal our blemishes

We are the men that teach our sons not to respect women

Sneaking glances at the swim suit addition

Telling Mary she is less of a woman until she is married

Confining women to the kitchen

We are the parents that show our kids that you don't have to

respect everyone

The broken "Brought it on themselves"

The burdens "Just not today"

The different that "Don't need **OUR** help"

The youth who are too young and naive to help

We are the stereotype we live down to

"Hehe it's okay, I'm just a blonde"

We are the consumers

"Well it's okay if only I buy from China"

We are the unappreciative

"If only I had the new..."

We are society

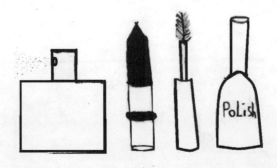

Elephant in the Room

Depression sits in the middle of the dinner table in the rosewood

red antique looking vase my cousin gave me

    -or maybe it is the vase itself.

It blocks the direct view of my family all sitting together joyfully

    -but it's okay I guess.

        No one seems to mind the separation.

The vase has a few chips but it still accomplishes the task at hand.

Still tells my mom that she shouldn't touch my shoulder in

attempts to comfort me.

Tells dad I don't like hugs from men anymore. Still reminds them

my innocence was sacrificed to make room for adulthood. I have

been thrown into distress so many times it taught me how to swim.

    -Or at least not show the signs that I'm drowning.

Still reminds them to make sure all the knives are hidden well.

    -Make sure they aren't tucked under my pillow at night.

It reminds us that some days I can't be left alone.

Depression mocks me when we I drag the fork to my mouth.

Every time I eat the utensils get heavier.

The body composition number that my 6th grade PE teacher gave

me,

questions every bite I put in my mouth,

-counts the calories before I swallow them.

Adds them to the pounds I have left to loose. Every time I lose a

pound I want to lose two more.

Like my weight isn't proportional to myself.

-Like skinny never feels skinny enough.

Depression is the family member visiting from out of town,

-the ones that don't talk to me anymore.

The ones who stopped coming to thanksgiving dinner because they

are tired of the small talk.

I have become the Elephant in the room.

I try to reduce my size

26

-so I'm not in their way.

I hear them whispering my name

with shushed voices that only mean shame.

Talking about things I won' talk about.

Places I no longer go.

They see *pink elephants* in their intoxicated glances.

I take up too much space in their *elephant* sized glances.

I want to clear my memory but

An Elephant Never Forgets.

Certified

Heart Breaker

"I am scared to love you because

Love requires falling and

I am afraid of heights."

Why You Should Date a Writer

If you date a writer,

      you'll never die.

Your image will be imprinted

      in her handwriting.

Your opinion will edit her words

      even when she doesn't agree with you.

Every color she writes about

      will reflect the color of your eyes,

She will compare everything

      to the feelings you once gave her.

She will write of heartbreak

      until she forgets how to spell pain.

If you date a writer,

      she will translate your portrait to English.

She has over 1000 words to describe your image.

She will put your smile in all her sunsets.

If you date a writer,

      you'll never have a dull day.

She will jolt awake with a new idea for a line/chapter

      and will want to tell you.

You will be the main character in all of her stories,

      so you must live according to the playbook she writes.

If you date a writer,

      she will find beauty in everything you do .

The weird scar on your elbow will tell a tale of the battle when the

stairs wrote their battle cry on your skin.

The tips of your anxiety bitten nails will be the curvy waves of the

      tsunami ridden waters of Australia.

If you date a writer, you'll never die.

Your image will be imprinted

      in her handwriting.

Your opinion will edit her words

 even when she doesn't agree with you.

Every color she writes about

 will reflect the color of your eyes,

She will compare everything

 to the feelings you once gave her.

She will write of heartbreak

 until she forgets how to spell pain.

If you fall in love with a writer, you'll never die

 but regret will make you wish you did

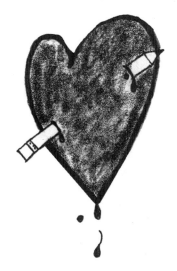

Pretty Boy

When I lay on your chest, your heart white-outs all the noise

      brushes my worries under the rug.

The sound of its beating, beats away the war inside of me until my

vocabulary can only mutter the words

      You are beautiful.

You're beauty is an unattainable kind of pretty.

A pretty that no boy can can get through the state of nirvana.

The kinda pretty that doesn't make you a pretty boy but

      -a beautiful one.

When your hand laces through mine, I feel like it becomes the

corset holding me together in a bondage

      -I cannot receive from any other person.

Your arms around me force my broken pieces back together with

the glue of your love.

Your words slide out of your mouth so eloquently

I wish I could just dance with them for awhile longer without you

doubting your excellence and burying your words under the

anxieties you told yourself were true.

I wish I could find the person that convinced you,

      you were anything but extraordinary.

 Make them see moon in stars because they can't see the moon and

stars

      you put into my sky every night after you say goodnight

followed by my name that your tongue paints so beautifully,

      lighting up the sky you created for me.

You brighten my everyday. I wish I could convince you that a day

spent with you is my new favorite day.

      -Besides the day we met, because

that's when I realized my sky's were dark without your smile and your star gazed eyes.

I love you was a lie I used to tell people.

Yes I cared, but love didn't exist before

You contacted me to help me see love through a new lens.

When I say I love you, I hope you don't take it lightly.

That was the first time, outside of family, that those words weren't

a lie.

 I tell my friends about you.

-My diary is tired of hearing your name.

But I can never get tired of hearing your name.

-Your name is very beautiful yet common but

its only beautiful when I know its connected to you.

When my friends called you a pretty boy

I couldn't explain to them how you're more than just pretty to me.

You are beautiful

Should I? (Potato-Head)

Should I tell my lover how vulnerable I am?

Should I tell him that I shake when I am about to let my heart out

of its rib cage?

Using my throat as a canal that's clearance way is a too

short for my words to fit in through. So they bump and stutter until

all my anxieties get caught in the back of my throat and

-I can can cannot let them out.

Should I tell him I had quite a fall

-that none of the kings doctors could put me back together?

Should I tell him I am obsessed with cats?

-because cats don't ask why I'm always sad

-nor do they care if I'm clingy.

They don't ask why I plant myself on the couch and use the light

from the TV to help me dig my roots a little deeper because

I can't get the light from the sunny side of things.

Eat popcorn every night hoping maybe if I eat enough of the seeds

I can grow as tall as the corn stalks so

    -I am no longer the short friend.

Should I tell him that I am sorry apologize too much?

Should I tell him I'm afraid of potatoes?

    -knowing he won't believe me until he chases me around

        the house until I'm in tears

Should I tell him that I try to stuff him like a turkey so

    -I can show him how thankful I am for his presence

Should I tell him that I love him?

    Should I tell him about the

scars that I don't feel like

explaining?

Should I tell him that I'm sorry?

Should I tell him that I love him?

Should I tell him I'm sorry I love him?

Insecure Hearts

If I say the words *I love you*

    -would you write them on your skin.

Show them to the world,

    -instead I hiding them within

If I say the words *I miss you*

    -would you smile with joy

Or maybe just laugh

    -and pretend to be coy

If I say the words *I need you*

    -would you think I need friends

Maybe you'd think I'm clingy

    -And tell me it needs to end

If I tell you *I'm in love with you*

    -would you look into my eyes

Perhaps you've fallen too

    -Or maybe its time for goodbyes

If I tell you *I am broken*

    -would you hold my hand

Tell me I'll be okay

    -and that you understand

How To Hide a Love That's Meant To Be

When they tell you his love is too young and fragile, *Don't argue.*

They won't understand that the same love is inside you.

When they tell you that this is only temporary you must believe

this moment has a near expiration date. Lock yourself up in the

past. Save all his messages and post them on your wall so you can

count down the days until your sentence is over.

Every time he called you beautiful,

> *is a day you have to stay in these crammed quarters.*

Keep the spreadsheet that proves your love is the purest form.

> *Even science says you have chemistry.*

Don't let them know you calculate your compatibility in math

class. *Find all the right angles in this love triangle. Calculate the*

probability that he might find his X and leave you wondering Y.

Carve his initials on all the pencils you use to write love songs with

> *so the only word you can write is his name.*

Cook every single meal you love.

Sprinkle his affection in the batter

so you can't escape the taste of him.

Plant pieces of him in your life so

you require his sunlight to give you energy.

Sew his name on all of your personal belongings.

Hug every time you see him so

you can remember what its like to be so close to someone

-you'll never have

Ration your compliments. He mustn't be hungry for your love.

Don't feed the idea that this will be over soon. He must not believe

its true, you don't want him to miss you.

You don't want him to hurt the way you do.

Love knows no darkness,

You can't put Love in a closet.

The thing with hiding a love that's meant to be is

You Can't

How to be Friends With Your Ex-Boyfriend's Mother

1. Don't mention his name. Don't mention him at all because when you do, you will start to see his image in everything she does. You will notice his chin and nose on her girly figure. You will notice his mannerisms in her smile. You will hear his laughter echoing through her vocal chords. Strumming the way he does when you give in to his fart jokes.

2. Don't make her laugh because it's clear where he got his humor from. When she shows you an old video he sent you, pretend it is the first time you have seen it so you don't have to explain why you didn't laugh. Try not to give yourself away with your silent tears. Don't try to get her to turn it off because her favorite part is

41

coming up. And you know exactly which one is her favorite.

3. Don't bring her to the place where he left you. You might mistake her silhouette as his. Her baggy sweater as his strong arms. You might think he is coming back to you in all the ways you know he won't. Like when she walks up you will rewind the day he dumped you. Imagine him walking back to his car, driving home, uneat the dinner she cooked him, work out so hard he stops sweating on the yoga mat you once shared, rewind so far back he doesn't recognize your name anymore.

4. Don't bring her to his favorite restaurant, because he always ordered what his mother suggested on the menu. You will see her put just as much salt as he does only tapping a bit in her palm. Sprinkling it over her steak until she dumps the rest of it on anyway. Followed by more salt. She will order unsweet tea even

though she lives in Texas because that's the way she always liked

it. The way she made it when he was growing up

5. Don't ask about the family because she knows that's your way of

asking about him. Asking if he passed the class he was worried

about, have gotten in a car crash from texting and driving again,

seeing if he has any recent lovers. Don't ask what college he is

going to because everyone knows how much you hate astronomy

and think it's a waste of time and money. There is no point in

going to his stupid school. You know he will make himself so busy

he forgets to look at the stars he choose to study. You won't run

into him in the hall so please don't mortgage your future on a

tuition debt fueled by the friend zone.

6. Don't look through her Facebook. Don't look through her pictures because you will run into him again. Get caught in the web and go through all her albums until every time you close your eyes at night you see his face. His 4yr old face baking cookies for the first time. Then accidentally like a photo from 5 years ago... And she will know immediately because she doesn't leave Facebook. She will know what you have done.

7. Don't ask her to go to the movies with you. She will drive to the movies using the same old back road no one knows about, she will butter her popcorn until it looks like cereal. She will choose the movie he can't stop talking about. You will be going on a date with him again. With his mother's body. And that is a new level of creepy ex-girlfriend.

8. When she asks if you would like to come over for dinner, lie and

say you have other plans. You don't want to see him sitting there

looking at you like he did when he drove off that day. When he

said it wasn't you it was him. You don't want to see his favorite

couch, the clothes he leaves in the living room, his shoes neatly by

the door, the only thing he keeps clean.

9. When you go out and someone calls her your mom don't object.

Just let them think that. Consider her your mother in law. The

woman who birthed the boy who ran away with your heart. Just let

it be. Don't try to explain to them that she is your lovers mom.

They won't understand the bond you share.

10. When she shows you family pictures from the Christmas party

you were supposed to attend, pretend not to notice the

photoshopped girl he has under his arm. The body she obviously worked on just as much as he worked on his. Don't envy her. Don't

think of the scenarios that could have happened if that were you.

Don't think of the tree behind them as the one you had a picnic

under last summer. Pretend not to notice their matching necklaces

that are a lot cooler than the ones you got him. When his mom

offers you a copy of the picture, take it. Throw it away in the trash

can he ran into on your second date.

You don't want to show her you still love him.

Beauty Queen

I want to feel beautiful again

I want him to remember my hair as the shiny satin that he used to

run his hands through.

    His knuckle's dents getting caught in the tangles of me.

I want him to remember my skin's edges and curves like a treasure

map he never got to explore. Some holes and markings.

I want him to remember my laugh like the play back of his favorite

song. Remember the days when we were in his first car,

    his hand laced in mine as he drove.

I want him to remember the taste of my kiss like southern sweet

tea in the middle of July. I want him to remember my eyes like a

river he got to look to see his own reflection in, dip his toes in my

love just barely rippling the surface of my embrace

But all I can think is:

My hair's a shade lighter than the muddy bath water that has been

forgotten in the old, beaten bath tub. Just silently waiting to be

drained

My embrace must taste like home squeezed juice that is half

between freshly made and strong hillbilly moonshine.

My eyes are like the little plastic jewelry girl's through away after

realizing they will never really be a princess. Old, tattered and

worthless.

I want to feel beautiful again but

I am just an old bedtime story he will tell his kids one day.

The Boy I Planted into Home

I forgot which human shaped box I left my heart in.

To whom did I leave my happiness with?

Where can I find the man who took my breath when I wasn't looking,

hid it in the places of me too dark to search in?

Am I not transparent yet?

Have I not became the ghost that hides in your closet until it is safe

to haunt you?

Have I not become the thin coating of masks I keep as skin?

 I remember-not to whom I gave my heart.

Where shall I find the boy I blossomed into a man?

Which body did I plant confidence in?

I have come to take the fruit I have sewed.

Labored.

If you build a man out of your composted rotten lies of love

Can he still bare fruit sweet enough to live on?

Where is the boy I would nourish with the strength

I scraped up that day.

Where is the boy in which I invested my future in?

Is he not here for the harvest?

Is he not ready to fulfill his promises of forever?

Where is the one in which my heart belongs?

Where is the man I nested into home?

Certified Heart Breaker

I have been a certified heart breaker since the first grade.

I remember waltzing in on Valentines day and placing myself on

my perfectly festive chair.

I watched as my girl classmates eyed Junior,

     -the cutest boy in school

They watched him parade around the classroom before handing me

an elegant gift basket

     -accompanied by a balloon and a smile.

Oh the looks I got!

     Girls glared at me tried to put holes in my happiness.

I gave them a warm smile

     -to declare my dominance over them

The ironic part is I didn't even like him

     -but I craved the taste of power that could only be

quenched by shattered hearts

Every year since, I have gotten special gifts from potential victims:

Teddy bears, flowers, candy...

-a box of chocolate on my door step with an invitation to a

party at his mansion on the lake

I am a certified heart breaker.

I wrap my words in verbal bacon

-that no man

-nor woman can resist.

My eyes are a siren luring a pirate

-before drowning them in her merciless waves of affection

Now that I am older,

Valentines day has become Bae Hunting season.

I am a ninja dodging cupid's arrows

-as they shoot everyone around me.

I have more phone numbers than a phone book.

-Get more dates than a calendar.

The president can't even get a hold of me!

As I walk down the street, everyone is staring at me.

-I don't even have to work out!

I have a PhD in L-O-V-E.

I am a certified heart breaker and you better watch out!

The Beast I Inherited

"They ask me how I fall in love with the worst of men. I leave my heart open for them. Why lock your door when you don't feel you have anything valuable left to steal?"

Loading Poem

This poem is about effects of Cyber Bullying

I have merged with my phone.

I don't know where my fingertips end and where the glowing

screen begins. I set the device in an empty room safely away from

people on its charger so it doesn't die.

    -I don't need anymore of my friends dying.

I plug myself into my phone so hopefully I don't die.

    Or just stop working today. *I just stop working sometimes.*

Can't turn on, maybe my light is too dim or my volume is on mute.

Notifications are turned off because I don't want to know who

wants to casually talk over coffee next week.

I can't seem to reset my system, so I close down all my windows so

no one can view `My History. Refresh` the page until I can see

my life clearly. I have caught a virus or two,

    -blurred the line between happy and sad.

Someone hacked into my *Motherboard* and recoded me to think

everyone is dangerous. I set up passwords to keep everyone out but

no one can seem to remember the sequence to get back in.

Maybe if I *hibernate* for a few days everyone will just leave me

alone. Don't spend time with me, don't attach your *hard drive*

or I will transfer my virus to you.

    -I have attachment issues.

Too many files stored in *My Memory*.

When I update my system I end up losing *Myself*.

Friendships keeps opening and closing they must be a virus

too.

Restrict their access so they can't see into my dirty life that I've

thrown into the *recycling bin*

Control Function Delete
Control Function Delete
Control Function...
I can't *Control* or *Function* so I *delete all my tasks*

because I cannot seem to *manage* them.

Control ALT Delete. Task Manager. Select All.

Delete.

My mind runs slower than *Internet Explorer* because

I downloaded too many emotions.

Pop up adds now fill my database.

"Eat less! Drink more! Get skinny fast"

"Buy this concealer to conceal the ugly parts of yourself

no one can love."

I close them down and the same empty black screen of death

haunts me everyday.

`Html code opening tag angle bracket`
`<depression>`

I can't remember how to close the tag.

The online forums never seem tell me how to be happy because

they are filled with trolls telling everyone to just to *shut down*

their system...

So I follow their instruction manual. *Close the tab*

labeled

`Life.`

Error virus: 404 Hope not found

Are you sure you want to open Bottle?

Self Control is not a trusted site

Body has stopped working

Error virus

Pills

Error

Overload

System Overdrive

System shut down.

Game over.

Rebooting.

Loading

Trouble shooting

Saving data

Wait I didn't call tech support I didn't want

Saving

Loading

Rebooting.

Loading

System update: Medication

System update: Life

Repairing hard drive

Relocation: Psych ward

System loading

Refreshing

Would you like to restore all previous tabs?

Obituary

I am sorry she's gone

    -Pushing daisies in a better place.

I am sorry she took her own life

Her parents will claim it as an accident.

Like they didn't see it coming. We'll just go with that.

    She swallowed the pills to numb the pain.

    -Just like the bottle told her to.

    Extra strength.

She never did have motivation or strength to get to get out of bed.

    That's why she took them, right?

She needed strength, *couldn't do it without the support.*

Took the whole bottle to make up for the times when she didn't

take any meds. because they told her its all in her head.

    -It's just a phase though.

58

She always liked the smell of bleach.

Must have mistaken it for the clear liquid she kept in her water

bottle. Always smelled like disinfectant. Like she

-Tried to kill the illness living in her mind.

It made her wobble when she walked,

taught her to speak in cursive

so her words would be beautiful enough to pay attention to

-but that's just what kids do these days.

She always liked guns.

Wore all black to camouflage with the barrel,

-maybe that's why you didn't see it against her head

-when she pulled the trigger.

She made necklaces as a child,

maybe that's why they found her with a rope around her neck.

She was hanging from the ceiling.

-You always did tell her to

"hang in there."

She fell asleep in the bath tub

with an alcohol level 4x the legal limit.

She's a minor

-That's normal though.

She always fell asleep in weird places

-because her thoughts kept her up at night.

Teenagers always need more sleep though,

-It gets better.

-Best days of your life, better.

Just following her friends

-Its normal, everyone feels like this.

They will claim it as an accident

-She did it for attention, right?

If she needed attention so bad,

then why didn't you give it to her?

How can you say you did not see this coming?

She quit doing everything she loved.

-She became a quitter.

She even carved her resignation on her wrists

on her body she tallied the days she had left.

How can you say you didn't see it coming?

She said it was coming

Vacation

I need a vacation from my mind.

I need to escape the icy parts of my brain that have only been

touched by the burning whiskey that trickles down my throat,

slides into my heart drowning my thoughts in a burning sensation

    -of relief.

Wishing the whiskey will be the suitcase that will support me

when my mind becomes a titanic tragedy.

    Sailor Jerry is the captain of my ship.

During my pursuit to happiness I get blindsided and

my mood sinks

    -unexpectedly.

I become consumed by an unforgiving weather of comments.

Look at the fatty, is she eating again?

    You're just another burden.

You're only a body and a pretty face.

    You're easily replaceable you stupid ditz.

Debating.

Whether I should get help or just wait until spring comes and

defrosts the cold shoulder I have given anyone

who reaches out to help me.

Maybe autumn will be better.

When I can fall like leaves off a tree and

camouflage myself in the leaves.

-well leaving of people

They're tired of me being sick of tired people thinking sickly.

-I am tired

They say I need to leave I just think...

I need a vacation from my mind.

I need the butterflies in my stomach to come out of hibernation.

They are in the cave I have kept them fearfully hostage in.

Scared one day they might find love and leave me.

Not to mention they're starving

not only because I refuse to feed them

-or myself for that matter

but also because they haven't felt important since his lies entered

my ears and escaped through the blood on my forehead after he

slammed me into a locker

For the 4th time that month.

Luckily, I didn't need stitches.

Luckily, the witnesses didn't care to tell me it wasn't normal

Luckily, I don't remember why he was mad.

His anger explodes like a landmine

      I didn't know I had to look out for.

On a battlefield I mistaken as

      -home.

The explosion rattles me again and is silently banging my brain.

      Telling me I need to break up with him again.

Telling me I can do better.

Telling me he is the only person who could love a girl with more scars then friends.

A girl with more luggage than love

I need a vacation from my mind

      -But I can't afford the hidden baggage fees

Home

My body is my home.

-My source of comfort and stability.

I keep the gate locked with three locks but I keep one unlocked

-so its a puzzle to enter my life.

I laugh so no one can hear the gates opening in sorrow.

-I use it as a moat

just in case the few guests that make it in,

-try to touch me.

I keep the **standard** almond fence pieces close together so you can't

see in.

-I like to keep my **standards** untenability high.

You can barely see the small house I have carefully hidden,

even when standing in my yard.

You can see a beautiful garden between the

cracks in my fence posts

-if you angle your head just right.

I have placed my hobbit sized door between

my shoulder and *waste*

I like watching the creatures scurrying around the bird bath

-located four memories away from my elbows.

Just follow the rows of roses with the sharpest thorns to the door.

-They are next to my funny bone

Only if I tell you of my entrance, you will find the door but

don't touch the paint.

-*It's wet.*

I spent months scrapping the walls clean of his fingerprints.

I washed away his scent with the garden hose

located in my tear ducts.

I tried to paint over his words.

I made a bonfire out of the clothes he left in the memory

-we used to watch TV in.

I tried to ring him out of my house but if you listen closely,

his laughter still echo's in the hall

like a song I can't take off loop.

His reflection has stained the bathroom mirror.

-I cant scrub him out of the tiles.

I tried to change the wallpaper

-but its never enough.

I don't recognize the building I wake up in

-I don't know how to leave these walls.

I don't know how to check the mailbox for your letters so

-I never respond.

I can't abandon my body,

my home,

my life.

I cant leave, because

I'm the only one that bothered to stay

Prescription for Friendship

I'm tired.

Not only from a lack of sleep but from a deep sickness of people.

I'm tired of people being sick of my illness.

They get mad at me for symptoms I have clearly stated.

Warning labels and fine print I have read to you.

You blindly accepted the terms and conditions.

Checked the box and forgot to unsubscribed to my latest *issues*

Is *Her Friendship* right for you? Taking her

-to social events

might cause her a loss of appetite, headaches, loss of speech and

perhaps dizziness, shakiness and noxiousness'.

Avoiding social events however might induce

loneliness, exclusion, loss of appetite, unusual sleep

patterns, or outbursts of panic attacks.

If you notice any concerning habits, please consult her doctor before letting her continue. If you take *Advantage* please do not start *Friendship*, it will cause suicidal thoughts or actions. If you have symptoms of arrogance, lack of empathy, or angry outbursts please consult *Patience* before considering if *Friendship* is right for you. Use with caution and moderation

Take daily for better results.

Offer expires in 5.6 seconds but will be offered again shortly due to indecisiveness

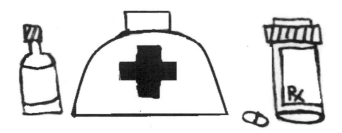

The Beast I Inherited

Growing up I was taught to mimic good behavior and live up to the legacy of the previous generations.

My cousin Tiffany was the mold I had to wedge myself inside of,

cutting off the extra pieces of me to shape my life like hers.

The dinner table was the first stage she performed at.

Her newest success was always on the menu.

Words filled her mouth as we learned to chew and swallow as she spoke. Her words had a performance that left no time for her to inhale our applause.

A GPA above 4.0 came easily to her.

She did rocket science for fun

Volunteered full time at the animal shelter

She stood at 5'10 104lbs

you could play xylophone on her rib cage,

Her wrists were so small

    even hair ties slid down them,

Her fingers kissed the back of her throat

    left calluses on her knuckles of her practiced profession.

Her belly memorized the echo of an auditorium

    knew to silence itself before the production

Knew not to say a word while she sat at the dinner table

    still "full" from eating an egg the morning before.

In 2009, my mom sat me down to tell me Anorexia left my Barbie

doll cousin in the hospital.

I didn't know what anorexia was

    but it sounded like a dinosaur.

This monstrous beast ate her away until she was too thin to walk.

    Her chopstick legs couldn't stand any longer.

      The water flooded her insides

left her drowning from the inside out.

The hospital bed gave her no place to perform her

successes stories.

She couldn't distract the doctors with her sugar coated words

She watched the secret trick in her disappearing act be known

by all the EMT.

They saw recipes she kept tucked beneath her skeleton.

They could read the dialect on her skin.

She recovered

Slowly gain her strength back,

her secret message no longer inside of her.

She performs 3x a day now

by doctors orders.

She has no menu to choose from,

her meals have been planned and portioned

She knows she can't be a skeleton girl anymore,

she must stay in a frame that would not pass as

Thinspiration,

eating only enough to keep her shadow large enough to

cast over me

Seven years later

I learned how to keep myself out of the hospital while

getting similar results.

I stand before you in a fraction of my original size,

yet too big to trigger any concerns.

My family must be so proud.

I grew up to be

Just like

Tiffany.

Awk ♡ Word

When they asked me why I write so many
sad poems I responded, "I love literature
more than I love myself that's why I
exchange pieces of my heart for poems
disguised as memories. "

Dear Santa,

I have been really good this year.

I went to work everyday I was scheduled,

all my siblings are still alive and

my parents have most of their hair.

For Christmas, I want happiness

A year subscription to joy

I hope they will give me free samples and tips on how to be happy.

 I want friends who will be antisocial with me.

Send Pintrest pins to each other when we are forced to be in the

same room and awkwardly avoid each other at HEB.

For Christmas, I want a boyfriend.

Now I know what you're thinking,

I got one last year.

-I think you sent me the wrong one.

I asked for a guy who is tall, broad shouldered, and buff, who is a

poet, athletic and musician.

I know, its a lot to ask for and he probably doesn't exist if he

doesn't,

-I want a pony.

Yours Wishfully,

Kayla

REPLY:

To: Kayla From: Santa

He already has a boyfriend.

What color do you want your pony?

Dear Princess Fiona,

As a child I always wanted to be a princess like Cinderella or

Aurora. But now that I'm older I can relate more to you.

You are the one that prince charming fell for.

The one who was so beautiful in the day time

-you made the blue flowers with red thorns look insignificant.

You had a voice so soft and sweet that you could put any man in a

trance. But when your skin got a taste of the moon,

it turned green, threw up any self confidence you gathered that

day. You turned into an ugly, self loathing, ferocious beast.

Don't get me wrong, I am not putting you down.

You were born with it.

Your parents sent you far away hoping you will get better soon.

   -Maybe you will grow out of it.

But darling, we both know better.

This isn't a phase.

"Only the kiss of true love will set you free is what they tell you.

You just need to try to be happy, they say.

But true love didn't turn out like you wanted.

A face, that looked like your biggest fears waltzed into your castle

and demanded you come with him.

He didn't sweep you off your feet and kiss up to your crap.

Fiona, you and I are a lot alike.

During the day, prince charming swoons over me asking me to

accompany him. I write so beautifully, I could make the swamp

water sound like birthday cake.

But I too get ugly when the moon starts to shine.

I get to be this hideous, self loathing, ferocious beast.

My happiness transforms into doubt and I can't see the light.

-I was born with it.

My friends all pushed me away hoping

-I would get better soon.

Maybe I will grow out of it.

-I just need to try to be happy.

But we know better.

I will not escape myself until I accept my ugly and move on.

Thank you Fiona for always being on my team. Teaching me that

not all princesses are blonde, size 3 beautiful.

Princesses aren't always happy.

Dear Fiona, thanks for never giving up and staying true to yourself.

Sincerely,

Your Biggest Fan

My God

Blood stained hands and satin colored lips

I am standing against the bridge.

No walls or windows in this deceiving tunnel

Not knowing how I got here

No walls or windows for people to see the savage beast

    locked in this skin.

They can't see the confusion painted on my interior walls.

Can't see the pain that holds me captive.

Alone in a world of greatness, not a sheep in sight.

I am amongst the wolves and martyrs

For there are only two types of people in this world.

I wear an arrangement of emotions on my sleeve.

I change into them often. I have one for every occasion

Although, I don't always know how to use them.

Not knowing if I am wolf or a martyr I pick up every mask I come

across.

These faces weigh me down

What can be greater than this burden I carry?

My shoulders cave in to the pressure of the world

Unable to move in faith,

I blindly follow the masses and forget to whom I belong.

My stubborn gratitude makes me stumble upon the rocks

        -the ones that are supposed to ground me.

Crushing the opportunities with my hateful words and arrogance

            I fail to notice the one to whom I belong.

On a journey to success I can't see past my finger tips.

They have clouded my mind with their air.

They leave the stench of smoke in bedded in my brain cells.

I follow the masses to what they call eternity.

Stumbling trembling down into the depths of hell.

I descend into my future.

I can taste the devil's cackle on my tongue.

He offers me the right hand of his throne.

I have kissed sins feet,

Memorized the lies of conduct.

I have submitted

I am lost in the masses.

Oh God, why hast thou abandoned me?

Where is my all powerful king?

Nothing is worse than this numbness!

For death where is your sting?

For even death tastes better than this bitterness.

Oh God, where is the one I once called Home?

To where is the one who held me when I was low?

Oh Lord, for how long will the wicked triumph?

For low long will I be lost?

For who will rise against these evil doers?

Who will save me from the masses?

Have I strayed away too far?

Have I already sold my soul to the devil?

Oh who will save me from the masses?

For who can overcome this wickedness I have become?

My God,

Oh My God,

I shall give you my breath in exchange for your blessing.

My God,

Oh My God,

Save me from this misery.

A hand reaches for my shoulder and

I began to float up into the clouds.

This pit is no longer my prison. For my burden has been lifted.

My masks have all burned. I have but one name I call my own.

The burden on my shoulders is no longer.

My Abba has heard my cries.

My Abba has carried me back home.

For I was once lost but now I have been found.

For I now lead the masses to my father,

No longer lost in the fog

He came and gave me his son to guide me.

No longer lost in the masses I cry

My Abba,

My God

for you have loved the most unlovable

Forever I will share your love for those who were lost

They can join us in our eternity.

Not for my glory but yours.

Not because you want me to spread religion but because

I want to share the love of this relationship.

Not to convert but to love.

My Abba,

My God

I am eternally grateful.

I Write Slams Not Tragedies

They say I need to make my poems into songs

so people can swallow the words.

Dilute the lyrics so they can drown it in the mainstream.

Sugar coat my sentences to give to kids that crave the truth their

parents have kept hidden in the cookie jar.

Off limits.

Put them on a diet that is limited to

the organic crap their parents listened to or

drink Pop melodies until they throw up the lyrics in their lifestyle.

They sound so bubbly but they burn coming back up.

Our songs telling girls to throw it back up.

My poems are raw and tender.

No need to peel back the electric guitars and base line

to get to the juicy center.

Over medium.

I want my words to have a strong taste they can't cure with milk.

Burn their tongue so the words will be

scarred in their mouth forever.

I am *lack-oh-s* intolerant,

Like I don't say *oh* when I have nothing better stay.

All of my words have meaning that won't be set on the back burner

until its in season.

These lines are c*austic,*

biting, acidic, sharp, full of cause yet so *divine*

Don't insult me by telling me to write my words into songs.

Don't bite off the hand that feeds you truth like the Gospel.

Literary Devices

I live the poetry I can not write.

I live between the semi colon and my overused transition word.

I cook breakfast for the *Personification* and the *Assonance* I am

housing for the month. They seem to like the meals I cook them

but they are hard to live with.

They never get along with *Literal* and *Travesty.*

Bickering whenever I am not looking.

They bully my conscious and word choice. I should really ask them

to leave but they're only staying for one more month.

Oxymoron was supposed to arrive last week but he's *always never*

on time. I don't know what to think of him.

He is a *paradox* of my liking and hard to accommodate for.

Satire bullies my words into submission until she can manipulate

my vocabulary into forming her sentences for her.

I always catch her sprinting through my *language loop*, pushing

over my stutter, arriving in my *Broca* and *Wernicke*.

She's always on my nerves.

Archetype is my favorite.

She and I are best friends, we finish each others

-Sandwiches

I just love the way she always knows what to say.

All these words are *crammed in my cranium and I can not*

continue to alliterate alternations any longer. I *can't accommodate*

for the *consonances'* that I am living with. I can't take these

crammed quarters.

I trip on my words they borrow then leave on the floor. I ran out of

literary devices that will teach me to speak in *College Professor.*

I try to house these words to make me seem more interesting and

intelligent but they just leave my mind a mess.

The End